This workbook be

_____

Fun and Fulfilling Careers One Question at a Time

Workbook

The companion workbook to the

Step-by-Step Guide to Thriving in Your

Personal and Professional Life

Heather H. Bennett

THREE SIMPLE STEPS FOR USING THIS WORKBOOK	3
CHAPTER 1	5
PERSONAL BRANDING BASICS	5
Building Blocks of a Personal Brand Diagram	6
Chapter 1 Exercises	*10*
S.M.A.R.T. Goals Image	13
CHAPTER 2 AUTHENTICITY: GET TO KNOW WHO YOU ARE AT YOUR CORE	15
Chapter 2 Exercises	*25*
CHAPTER 3 FIND YOUR INSPIRATION: LOOK BACK TO MOVE FORWARD	44
Chapter 3 Exercises	*45*
Time Map Diagram and Templates	57
CHAPTER 4 DISCOVER WHAT YOU LOVE TO DO: FINDING YOUR FAVORITE WORK AND LIFE ACTIVITIES	63
Chapter 4 Exercises	*66*
Your Personal Brand Statement	67
CHAPTER 5 CREATE YOUR FUTURE: DARE TO DREAM	70
Chapter 5 Exercises	*71*
CHAPTER 6 FIND YOUR PLACE: SEEK WHERE YOU ARE NEEDED IN THE WORLD	82
Chapter 6 Exercises	*83*
Job Post for Career Track Template	91
CHAPTER 7 CREATING YOUR STRATEGIC PERSONAL BRAND PLAN: SPECIFIC TASKS AND ACTIONS TO ACHIEVE YOUR IDEAL WORK AND LIFE	111
Social Media Pyramid Diagram	112
Chapter 7 Exercises	*118*
Elevator Pitch Components Diagram	130
Accountability Chart for Your Personal Brand Strategy	132
CHAPTER 8 KEEPING YOUR PERSONAL BRAND STRONG: CHECKUPS, MAINTENANCE, AND UPDATES	133
Chapter 8 Exercises	*137*
Pre-Networking Checklist	137
Social Media Checklist for Personal Brands	138
Timeline Planner Example	141
Acknowledgements	*145*
About the Author	145

Fun and Fulfilling Careers One Question at a Time: Workbook

Welcome

to the companion workbook for

Fun and Fulfilling Careers One Question at a Time

The purpose of the book and workbook are to help you create your personal brand so it reflects who you are, what you bring with you, where you are needed, and how you will get where you want to go.

Chapters 1, 2, and 3 questions and exercises guide you to discover your unique talents, skills, and personality traits – who you are at your core, your authentic self in the context of your past and present work, hobbies, commitments, and volunteer work.

Chapter 4 questions help you look back at your experiences to recognize the type of work and activities that truly bring you fulfillment.

Chapter 5 questions and exercises help you list the environment and circumstances that best fit your personal brand.

Chapter 6 questions and exercises were designed to research where a need exists in the world for your unique skills and talents.

Chapters 7 and 8 questions and exercises help you plan to reach your professional goals using your personal brand statement.

How to use this workbook

Each section of the companion book, *Fun and Fulfilling Careers One Question at a Time*, starts by discussing the concepts that help you get through each step to make your personal brand better, one question at a time. Read the chapters in the book and then make notes in the workbook.

Easy to follow exercises help you work through that chapter's concepts. Use this workbook to have a single, easy to review and store working document with lots of space for writing in your answers to the personal branding questions.

By having you write down on paper your responses to the questions and fill in the exercises, you will retain more of the knowledge you gain about yourself and what your future work and personal life could look like. It is worth your time and effort to try to do as many exercises as you can.

Three Simple Steps for Using This Workbook

1. Read the paragraphs at the beginning of each chapter of the companion book found on Amazon, **Fun and Fulfilling Careers One Question at a Time**.

2. **Answer the questions** and **complete the exercises** in the workbook.

3. Use the notes section of the workbook to take notes on what you want to remember most from each section of the book and insights you have gained into your career and personal goals.

The purpose of this workbook is to give you the tools and plans to get you to the life you want. Let's get started!

Part One:
Discovering and Building Your Personal Brand

How to Plan and Prepare for Your Next Career or New Challenge with Passion, Authenticity, and Hope

The purpose of this workbook and the companion book, *Fun and Fulfilling Careers One Question at a Time*, is to help you choose the life you need to be your best.

NOTES:

Chapter 1

Personal Branding Basics

What is Personal Branding?

Personal Branding is the skills, talents, personality traits and passions of an individual that are consistently communicated through all interactions with others, online and offline.

Why Should I Create a Personal Brand?

With every interaction we have with people around us, we leave an impression. Your personal brand is a guide to make sure you are intentionally communicating what you want others to understand about you and your message. An authentic personal brand allows you to focus on what business activities will give you fulfillment through meeting a need in the world.

NOTES:

_____
_____
_____
_____
_____
_____
_____
_____
_____
_____
_____
_____
_____
_____
_____
_____
_____
_____

How to Build a Personal Brand

Building a personal brand consists of the following building blocks: self-awareness, experience, opportunity, and a strategic plan.

Self-awareness is found through understanding the skills, personality traits, and talents that make up who you are at your core.

Experience is the combination of work, volunteer roles, and commitments that control and guide how you have spent and continue to spend your time.

Opportunity occurs after a combination of the research, expert interviews, and ideal job posts has been completed guiding you towards a future career or role.

The *strategic plan* lists the actions needed to fully utilize your personal brand through networking and connecting, continuous learning and maintaining your personal brand.

The exercises in this workbook will start you on your path for creating your personal brand. The diagram below shows how these discovery points are the building blocks of your personal brand.

Building Blocks of a Personal Brand Diagram

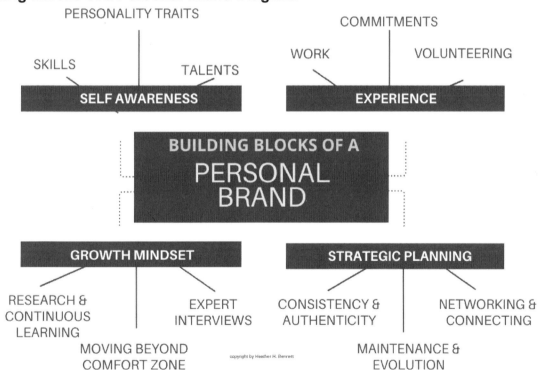

Planning is More than Half the Fun
Working on your personal brand to achieve your goals requires a lot of planning. The importance of the planning process should not be overlooked.

What tools and methods do you use for planning your week, month, and year?

NOTES:
_____
_____
_____
_____
_____
_____
_____
_____
_____
_____
_____
_____
_____
_____
_____
_____
_____

Self-Care for the Future

Practicing and scheduling self-care is important to prepare for the unpredictable. By creating self-care routines and habits, you are better able to focus on your personal brand, career, and goals.

Examples of self-care habits include:

- Plan and take vacations.
- Schedule medical checkups and follow the directions of your practitioners to keep you healthy.
- Workout and do post workout relaxation like a long shower, spa, or sauna.
- Meditate through mindfulness and breathing.
- Do at least one thing a day that makes you laugh and smile.
- Be grateful.
- Connect with others.

What self-care do you practice regularly?

What could you add or change to make it better?

NOTES:

The Gift of Journaling

Discovering your personal brand requires intense self-awareness. One tool to help with self-awareness is journaling. Journaling is a gift to yourself. Years or even months from now, looking back on what was most important or top of mind at the time gives your perspective on how you manage life, set, and reach goals as well as how to improve where you are currently.

What kinds of journaling have you done in the past? Did it work for you?

What type of journal appeals to you the most?

What are you most likely to consistently commit to?

_____
_____
_____
_____
_____
_____
_____
_____
_____
_____
_____
_____
_____
_____
_____
_____

Chapter 1 Exercises

Goals and Reasons

Congratulations! You have reached the first exercise.

This first exercise may be the most important one. It is designed to give you a guide and the motivation to go through and successfully complete all the other exercises and make it more fun and exciting in the process.

Reasons

For this exercise, write down why you are reading this book. Not why you think you should read this book but, for you personally,

Why are *you* reading this book? Be specific and detailed.

Why did you pick up this book?

What do you hope the book will do for you?

What is missing in your life?

What is the reason behind you needing a change in your life?

What has changed about you or the world around you that compels you to want more or need more out of life?

What about your life seems disconnected or out of tune?

What do you love or not love about your career or situation?

What challenges in your life do you want to resolve?

What challenges do you feel this book may clarify and help you overcome?

NOTES:

_____
_____
_____
_____
_____
_____
_____
_____
_____
_____
_____
_____
_____
_____
_____
_____

How to Set Goals

Think about and write down what goal or goals you hope to achieve during your time focusing on your unique and authentic personal brand. By having a clear goal in mind, you will more likely finish feeling a sense of accomplishment and joy.

Choose a goal that you can note and celebrate to acknowledge that you have grown as a person. Use the SMART method to create a goal that is Specific, Measurable, Achievable, Relevant and Timely. **S.M.A.R.T. Goals Image**

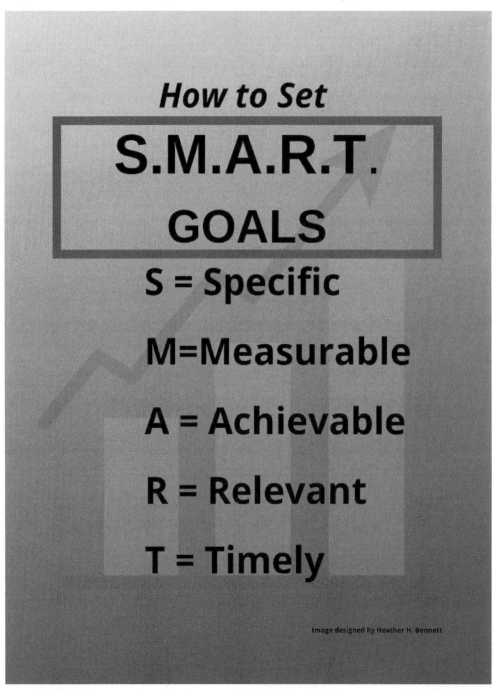

Fun and Fulfilling Careers One Question at a Time: Workbook

Your Goals

What are your Goals?

What event, action, or achievement must happen so that you feel you have truly made the effort?

What are you hoping to achieve?

Notes:

Chapter 2 Authenticity: Get to Know Who You Are at Your Core

Getting to know who you are and what you want to do takes time.

Imagine if you could take the time to plan how you want to spend your time.

What would you do?

What needs to change so that you can have more time to plan?

How can you make more time for yourself this week or this month?

NOTES:

_____

_____

_____

_____

_____

_____

_____

_____

_____

_____

_____

_____

_____

_____

What to Do if You Get Stuck

It happens. People freeze. The fight or flight response fails. We are stuck, confused, and wondering what to do next. This applies to these exercises, but it also applies to everyday life. Write down ways you could try each of these.

1. Think about the last time you felt calm, at peace, and relaxed. Close your eyes and imagine you are in that space and time. What does it sound or smell like? Mentally play over and over a 1-2-minute loop of the most relaxed moments. Take deep breaths and envision being there. Slowly tighten and release every muscle in your body starting with your toes and ending with your forehead, while laying or sitting still. Take 3 more deep breaths. Keep your eyes closed and imagine your relaxation space again. (Length of time is 5-10 minutes).

NOTES:

_____
_____
_____
_____
_____
_____
_____
_____
_____
_____
_____
_____
_____
_____
_____
_____
_____
_____

2. When does time fly for you? What activity makes you lose track of time, creating a sense of flow? (Flow is when one is completely focused on an activity so that they lose sense of time and are at the same time energized by the activity). Try to schedule an uninterrupted time to do this activity. Turn off your phone. Focus on the activity. If you must limit it to an hour, then do that but try to do it for at least an hour. (1-4 hours).

NOTES:

3. Do one uncomfortable thing. Walk instead of driving to the store. Call a friend of a friend that you would like to network with but have been waiting for the right moment. Eat a type of food you never have before. Listen to music you normally would not prefer. Read a book in a genre you don't typically buy or take out of the library. Try a different type of workout. Strike up a conversation with a stranger. By shaking up your normal routine, you will open various parts of your brain. (5-60 minutes).

NOTES:

4. Read a book. Not just any book. Read the book that you bought last year and meant to get to over the summer, but never did. Read the book your best friend or coworker loaned you and somehow forgot about in the shuffle of your home. Ask your roommate, spouse, kids, neighbor down the hall or other people you live with or near if they have a favorite book to lend you. This action actually works two-fold: it forces you to interact in a unique way with someone, it creates a situation where you will have to interact with them again to return the book and it gives you a discussion point to connect with them on it. Why are book clubs so popular? Besides the obvious food and beverage benefits, they allow us to connect with other humans. (5 minutes to 5 weeks).

NOTES:

5. Ask a close friend or sibling what they admire most about you. Simply hearing positive affirmations from someone you care about can change your entire outlook, giving you a safe and confident place to continue to work. My family plays a game during long car trips when the agitation level reaches a high point. We call it "Warm Fuzzies." It is especially useful at defusing the tension between siblings or exhausted parents and small children. The first person says something kind about another person in the car. Then, that person says something kind about another person and so on until everyone has had at least 2 positive affirmations said to them. Warning: this may take practice and you will get push back from the kids, especially teens. Also, beware of backhanded compliments. Funny and witty, yes! Kind? Not so much. (15 minutes – 1 hour).

NOTES:

6. Practice mindfulness. Wonderful apps, podcasts and online YouTube videos can guide you through mindfulness exercises. Try one to experience life in the moment… to truly be present. (5 or more minutes).

NOTES:

Knowing When to Leave or Say No

The work you are doing to learn more about yourself, your dreams, goals and more will take time. Finding time to do this important work may mean having to make hard choices.

What roles in your life can you step away from?

Here are some questions to ask yourself before deciding to step away from a role:

- What is the original reason you started this role/activity? Is it still a valid reason?

- Who will benefit from you staying?

- Who will benefit from you leaving?

Fun and Fulfilling Careers One Question at a Time: Workbook

- What roles in your life will benefit once you no longer are committed to this role?

- What roles need more attention and time from you that you are unable to give because of this role?

NOTES:
_____
_____
_____
_____
_____
_____
_____
_____
_____
_____
_____
_____
_____
_____
_____

Go Ahead and Brag About Yourself

Bragging within limits is necessary to your success, happiness, and growth as an individual. No one ever gets a positive response after a job interview without saying at least a few positive things about themselves.

List all the examples, success stories and accomplishments that could you brag about yourself. Be generous and keep adding to the list.

What are you proud of?

NOTES:

Fun and Fulfilling Careers One Question at a Time: Workbook

Chapter 2 Exercises

The set of exercises below will help you learn what *talents*, *skills*, and *personality traits* define you.

Note: These answers will be used later, so don't hold back on writing down as many answers as you can. Including a lot of answers will let you have many to choose from when you reach the later exercises.

Talents

Look back on yourself as a child, teen, and college student.

What did you love to do in your free time during weekends, summers, holidays, camps, and afterschool?

_____
_____
_____
_____
_____
_____
_____
_____
_____
_____
_____
_____
_____
_____
_____
_____
_____
_____

What hobbies, sports, household activities like cooking or organizing, crafts, arts – performing and/or media, collections, games, or other activities did you love to do? List as many as you can and draw pictures or diagrams if it helps.

Now looking at the list, write down the activities that you consider to be one of your top talents. List 5 things even now that you know you are genuinely good at and bring you joy:

1.

2.

3

4.

5.

Note any similarities in the activities listed above.

What do they have in common with each other?

Which one stands out from the rest? Put a box around it.

Circle the one that brings you the most joy.

Complete the following phrases to help you find your talents.

I have been told I am incredibly talented at…

My greatest talent is…

The one talent I am known for is…

Remembering Moments of Pride

Think of a time you felt immense pride: business, scholastic, sports, work, art, performance, or accomplishment. Having these carefully chosen and stored memories of a time of pride helps us when we doubt ourselves.

List moments when you felt immense pride in yourself.

Fun and Fulfilling Careers One Question at a Time: Workbook

Think of at least 3 times when your showed true talent.

Talent demonstration 1:

Talent demonstration 2:

Talent demonstration 3:

Now focus on the strongest memory. What talent did you show to earn that sense of pride? Feel free to draw a picture, chart, or diagram to explain. If you have a photo or trophy representing that time of pride, use a printout to help you remember.

___
___
___
___
___
___
___
___
___
___
___
___
___
___

Images and printouts to help you remember what to be proud of.

Skills

Skills are a list of abilities that you do well and that have been improved through use and study. Unlike talents, skills require practice, study, and education to become proficient.

The major difference between talents and skills is that skills require persistence of practice and study, whereas talents are innate and naturally show themselves without necessarily needing practice or study. You should be proud of the commitments you have made to learn and develop a skill.

The purpose of this exercise is to see what you bring to the table.

What are the unique skills that allow you to do your job, succeed at a task and make you a valuable contributor to a group, corporation, team, or organization?

_____
_____
_____
_____
_____
_____
_____
_____
_____
_____
_____
_____
_____
_____
_____
_____
_____

Below is a list of skills. Circle the ones that are most true for you.

Use the following sentence starters to help.

    I am very skillful at ….

    I am known for being good at…

    People know they can rely on my….

Fun and Fulfilling Careers One Question at a Time: Workbook

List of Skills

- Listening
- Adapting or being flexible
- Coaching or directing
- Reading
- Conflict resolution
- Maintaining focus
- Creativity
- Project management
- Following a recipe
- Perseverance
- Decision Making
- Delegating
- Doing laundry
- Hospitality
- Communicating
- Motivating
- Managing teams
- Mentoring others
- Shopping
- Problem solving or troubleshooting
- Strategic Thinking
- Cooking/baking
- Stress management
- Parenting
- Organizing
- Time management
- Research
- Fiscal management
- Performing repetitive tasks
- Critical questioning
- Following directions on a road
- Writing
- DIY home projects
- Teamwork
- Developing & maintaining relationships
- Taking initiative or action
- Presenting to a group
- Cleaning a home
- Driving
- Event planning
- First aid
- Budgeting
- Home decorating
- Computer or social media
- Sports
- Making people laugh
- Studying
- Travelling
- Caring for people or pets
- Fundraising

Add additional skills if needed:

Highlight Your Skills

Imagine participating in a team building exercise at work or on a reality TV show. What skills would you offer to make the team succeed? If it helps, think about yourself five to ten years ago. What skills have stayed the same? What have you added?

List 3 skills that you are good at and came naturally to you. These can come from the list above.

1.

2.

3.

NOTES:
_____
_____
_____
_____
_____
_____
_____
_____
_____
_____
_____
_____
_____
_____
_____
_____

List 3 skills that you worked hard to learn through education or persistent practice and are still confident in your ability to do them. Natural ability is wonderful, but some skill sets require learning and practice to master. Just because you had to work hard to be great at a skill, does not mean it is not a strong part of who you are.

1.

2.

3.

NOTES:

Personality traits

For this section, it is important to focus on traits you personally consider as positive. Ignore any negative thoughts or personality traits of which you are not proud. Part of understanding your authentic self is being aware of what personality traits will help you succeed and become your best self.

Below is a list of personality traits. Circle the ones that are most true for you.

Use the following sentence starters to help:

I can best be described as …

The words I think of when I look in the mirror are ….

Managers, team members or leaders have described me as….

_____
_____
_____
_____
_____
_____
_____
_____
_____
_____
_____
_____
_____
_____
_____

List of Personality Traits

Active or energetic	Educated	Loyal lovable
Admirable	Elegant	Methodical
Adventuresome	Eloquent	Meticulous
Agreeable	Empathetic	Moderate
Ambitious	Enthusiastic	Modern
Articulate	Extrovert	Modest
Athletic	Fair	Neat
Attractive	Faithful	Obedient
Authentic	Firm	Objective observation
Balanced	Flexible	Old-fashioned
Benevolent	Forgiving	Open
Calm	Friendly	Optimistic
Caring	Frugal	Organized
Cerebral	Fun-loving	Passionate
Challenging	Gentle	Patient
Charismatic	Genuine	Peaceful
Cheerful	Glamorous	Perceptive
Clever	Good-natured	Perfectionist
Colorful	Gracious	Persuasive
Compassionate	Grateful	Playful
Competitive	Hardworking	Polished
Confident	Healthy	Popular
Conscientious	Idealistic	Practical
Considerate	Imaginative	Principled
Contemplative	Independent	Private
Cooperative	Innovative	Protective
Courageous	Intelligent	Prudent
Courteous	Introvert	Punctual
Creative	Intuitive	Rational
Decisive	Kind	Realistic
Discreet	Liberal	Reflective
Dramatic	Logical	Religious
Dutiful	Loving	Resourceful

Respectful	Shrewd	Tasteful
Responsible	Simple	Thorough
Sage	Social	Tidy
Scholarly	Sophisticated	Tolerant
Selfless	Stylish	Understanding
Self-sufficient	Subtle	Urbane
Serious	Sweet	Vivacious
Sexy	Sympathetic	Warm

Personality Traits of Your Closest Confidants

List your four closest friends or trusted colleagues.

After each name, put three personality traits that describe that person.

Describe what you admire about their personalities. Focus only on the traits that are positive and hopefully you have seen help them succeed in their own lives.

Friends (personalities)

Your Friend's Name_____

Personality traits:

2. Your Friend's Name_____

Personality traits:

3. Your Friend's Name_____

Personality traits:

4. Your Friend's Name_____

Personality traits:

Looking over this list, are there any personality traits that you share with them?

Fun and Fulfilling Careers One Question at a Time: Workbook

List the personality traits you share.

Which personality traits do you share with one or more of them?

NOTES:

Create Your Core List

Next, gather the information in the previous exercises into one place using the Core List template below. Listing what you learned about yourself in the exercises above will help clarify who you are at your very core. You will create a core list that describes your authentic self.

Looking back on your answers to the earlier exercises, fill in the lists below.

Your Core List Template

My Top 3 Talents

1.

2.

3.

My Top 3 Skills

1.

2.

3.

My Top 3 Personality Traits

1.

2.

3.

Describe Who You Are

Using the top talents, skills and personality traits that define you, create a one to three sentence description of who you are.

Fun and Fulfilling Careers One Question at a Time: Workbook

Chapter 3 Find Your Inspiration: Look Back to Move Forward

This chapter is focused on helping you discover your favorite work and life activities.

How you spend your time can be divided into three activity categories: Work, Commitments, and Hobbies. Quickly fill in each category to keep track of how you spend your time.

Work

Commitments

Hobbies

Chapter 3 Exercises

Inspiration provides the needed boost to accomplish great things!

The exercises for Chapter 3 let you know which activities:

- stir your soul,
- inspire you to do and be more, and
- bring you great joy, satisfaction, and fulfillment.

Work & Volunteering Roles

List, with a brief description of your role, the last three to seven work positions or volunteer positions you have had and what you liked best and least about each. If it is easier, choose the positions that have had the biggest impact in your life.

Use the following template for each role or position for work or volunteering.

_____
_____
_____
_____
_____
_____
_____
_____
_____
_____
_____
_____
_____
_____
_____
_____
_____
_____
_____
_____

Role Template

Organization name:

Your role:

Your favorite part:

Your least favorite part:

What skills or knowledge you gained from the role:

Who you helped:

What achievements or results were accomplished through your actions (projects, goals, awards):

Role Template

Organization name:

Your role:

Your favorite part:

Your least favorite part:

What skills or knowledge you gained from the role:

Who you helped:

What achievements or results were accomplished through your actions (projects, goals, awards):

Fun and Fulfilling Careers One Question at a Time: Workbook

Role Template

Organization name:

Your role:

Your favorite part:

Your least favorite part:

What skills or knowledge you gained from the role:

Who you helped:

What achievements or results were accomplished through your actions (projects, goals, awards):

Role Template

Organization name:

Your role:

Your favorite part:

Your least favorite part:

What skills or knowledge you gained from the role:

Who you helped:

What achievements or results were accomplished through your actions (projects, goals, awards):

Fun and Fulfilling Careers One Question at a Time: Workbook

Role Template

Organization name:

Your role:

Your favorite part:

Your least favorite part:

What skills or knowledge you gained from the role:

Who you helped:

What achievements or results were accomplished through your actions (projects, goals, awards):

Hobbies

Hobbies exist purely for our pleasure and enjoyment. The smallest activity can be a hobby. Hobbies have been known to grow into businesses and careers, especially as the concept of always having a side hustle and multiple income sources become more prevalent.

First create an extensive list of all the hobbies you have done throughout your life. Next fill out the Hobby templates for your current top 3 hobbies.

List all the hobbies you have had throughout your life:

Fun and Fulfilling Careers One Question at a Time: Workbook

Talk about the hobbies you have now or wish you had more time for now.

Hobby:

What do you love about this hobby?

How did you discover or who helped you start doing this hobby?

Tell a story about the first time you tried this hobby or what events occurred that led you to make this an important part of your time.

When you are preparing to do this hobby, what inspires or excites you the most?

What is your favorite part about the hobby?

Hobby:

What do you love about this hobby?

How did you discover or who helped you start doing this hobby?

Tell a story about the first time you tried this hobby or what events occurred that led you to make this an important part of your time.

When you are preparing to do this hobby, what inspires or excites you the most?

What is your favorite part about the hobby?

Fun and Fulfilling Careers One Question at a Time: Workbook

Hobby:

What do you love about this hobby?

How did you discover or who helped you start doing this hobby?

Tell a story about the first time you tried this hobby or what events occurred that led you to make this an important part of your time.

When you are preparing to do this hobby, what inspires or excites you the most?

What is your favorite part about the hobby?

Commitments

Beyond our jobs and hobbies, a variety of activities take up our time and fill our days. In this exercise, focus on what takes up your time that did not fall into the categories listed above.

Think about how you spend your weeknights, weekends, and vacations.

What activities do you spend the most time doing?

What activities do you plan the rest of your day around?

Imagine you are looking at a calendar for your year, what are the items that come up most frequently?

What are the calendar events that make you smile/dread when you see them on next week's agenda?

_____
_____
_____
_____
_____
_____
_____
_____
_____
_____
_____
_____
_____
_____
_____
_____

Time Mapping (Mind Mapping Your Time)

In this exercise, you will use a mind map to visualize how you spend your time each year.

Categories to consider adding: your career, volunteering, each of the family members/others you are a caregiver for, pets, hobbies, activities, clubs, organizations you belong to, career planning (networking events), self-care (workouts, therapy, medical appointments), home care (bill paying, housework, home repair or scheduling).

After creating the major categories, create branches off each to further explain all the time usage needed for each part of your life. Finally, look at all the various parts of your life or career and consider what your life would be like without each part. Prioritize your favorites (and the one that pays the bills of course).

Which ones make you happy?

Which cause stress and anxiety?

Which ones have changed?

Have you changed so that certain categories no longer make sense to keep in your life?

Fun and Fulfilling Careers One Question at a Time: Workbook

Time Map

A Time map is a Mind Map that organizes your life on one page. Start by creating circles of the different parts of your life: work, family, hobbies, volunteering, etc. Next, create branches with the responsibilities that require your time for each one. Create this time map once a year to keep track of how you are using your time and learn where you want to change how to use your time in the future.

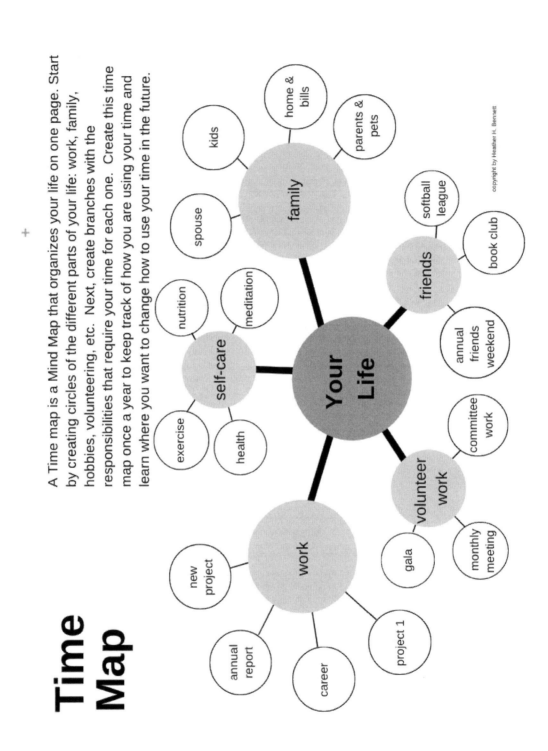

Time Map Diagram and Templates

Fun and Fulfilling Careers One Question at a Time: Workbook

Time Map dated_____

Time Map dated_____

Time Map dated_____

Part Two:
Researching, Finding and Preparing for Your Next Role

Often choosing a job that you love seems overwhelming because we are trained to follow logical career paths that stem from our education and past work experience. Separating your skills and talents from what is the logical next job in your career helps you to find new opportunities outside of what is typical. Try focusing on your skills and what other roles would use those skills.

Simply understanding what jobs await someone with your qualifications requires a little research. Research where you could go and then prepare for success once you get there.

What if - for most of the year - you could do what you love? What would that be?

_____
_____
_____
_____
_____
_____
_____
_____
_____
_____
_____
_____
_____
_____
_____
_____
_____
_____

Finding opportunities

During Part Two of this workbook, we will use your newly discovered core list and self-awareness to find opportunities in work, life and play that are authentic and fulfilling for you.

Chapter 4 helps you create a personal set of tools and strategies that will guide your search for a fulfilling career and life.

Chapter 5 helps you to dream about the possibilities that could be available to you.

Chapter 6 helps you research where your unique talents, skills, and personality traits are needed in a career, volunteer position, and/or hobby.

It is highly recommended to complete each chapters' exercises before beginning the next as they build upon the prior work.

Note: Each section contains a Lifestyle Track (focused on a hobby or lifestyle) as well as a Career Track (focused on jobs both paid and volunteer). You can do both Tracks at the same time if you choose.

Chapter 4 Discover What You Love to Do: Finding Your Favorite Work and Life Activities

Much of the work prior to this section required you to think hard about your life. Answer the questions below to help you stay grounded in where you are now as you prepare for the future.

Do you have a source of income to cover your basics needs?

What do you do for yourself?

How do you exercise, practice self-care, socialize, and have fun?

_____
_____
_____
_____
_____
_____
_____
_____
_____
_____
_____
_____
_____
_____
_____
_____
_____

Joy Creators

Personal joy creators are a toolkit for transforming a troublesome or uninspiring moment into energy.

What brings you joy?

_____
_____
_____
_____
_____
_____
_____
_____
_____
_____
_____
_____
_____
_____
_____
_____
_____

Some proven boosters of serotonin (your body's mood enhancing chemical) are reading, listening to music, coloring, doing puzzles, playing games, painting, or having a conversation with a friend, meditating, listening to music, exercising, and spending time in sunlight. For more examples, see Chapter 4 in *Fun and Fulfilling Careers One Question at a Time*.

Time management

With the rapid increase in the amount of information we are expected to process daily, how are we expected to find time for everything we need or want to do?

Time Management Tip 1: Just say NO!

What tasks can you say NO to this week?

Ask yourself these two questions before deciding what to say No to.
- Do I love and enjoy doing this?
- Does this task or activity directly help me towards one of my top three life goals?

Time Management Tip 2: Write it Down

What can you do to keep track of your to do list and stay organized?

Time Management Tip 3: Automate Your Life

How can you automate the everyday tasks of running your life?

Fun and Fulfilling Careers One Question at a Time: Workbook

Chapter 4 Exercises

Prioritizing your time

This exercise is about prioritizing what not only brings you joy, but also fulfillment. It may take a lot of time, but the real goal of this exercise is to learn what you truly want to keep doing.

Look at all the lists you have created on how you spend your time and evaluate each role, responsibility, and activity.

- ♥ Put a heart next to the three that you want to do every week for the next year. Don't be reasonable or think too hard about which ones you will choose. Imagine money and time and travel are not limitations.
- ☐ Put a box around the one thing you must do to support yourself and your family or the one/two you need to do to honor a commitment. Imagine all other commitments would no longer be obligations. Choose only one or two at most.
- ∗ Put a star next to the one that gives you the most pride and joy that you have not marked with a heart or boxed already.

List the 5 activities, roles, obligations, and hobbies you marked above.

Which ones are you passionate about, fulfilled by, and/or inspired by to live your life more completely?

1.

2.

3.

4.

5.

Fun and Fulfilling Careers One Question at a Time: Workbook

Create your Personal Brand

Now it is your turn to tell your own story.

Your Personal Brand Statement

Fill in the blanks below with your answers from all of the exercises you have completed.

Personal Brand for _____ (your name)

I am known for being really good at _____ (skill),

_____ (talent) and

_____ (skill/or/talent).

My friends and coworkers know they can expect me to always be

_____,

_____ and

_____ (personality traits).

Fun and Fulfilling Careers One Question at a Time: Workbook

I am passionate about ….

I feel inspired when I ….

I feel fulfilled when I ….

Finding Your Happy Place

This exercise is a simple visualization to help you create a memory tool that will calm you and comfort you when you are feeling stressed or uncertain.

List the places and moments you feel the happiest:

_____
_____
_____
_____
_____
_____
_____
_____
_____
_____
_____
_____
_____
_____
_____

Chapter 5 Create Your Future: Dare to Dream

For this chapter, you are invited to describe your dreams for an ideal future. The exercises help you list the specific environments and circumstances that you find most appealing.

Try one of these creativity tips this week to see if it inspires creativity in you. List how you could try these creativity tricks this week.

Creativity Tip 1: See, stream, or rent a movie. What media inspires you?

Creativity Tip 2: Break out the crayons and coloring books. What do you like creating artistically?

Creativity Tip 3: Take a hike. Look for art and architecture. Where could you go hiking?

Creativity Tip 4: Grab your passport. How can you experience a global viewpoint?

Chapter 5 Exercises

The exercises below will help you describe opportunities that attract you and make the most of your personal brand.

Passion & Strength

Find your passion. Ask yourself the following questions:

What am I deeply passionate about?

What topics do I love thinking, talking, learning, and reading about?

What subjects do you enjoy learning more about with respect to your future career?

Know Your Strengths

You have already listed talents and skills that you know you are good at. List these and focus on the ones that directly tie into what you are passionate about.

What talents/skills do I excel at, have I mastered, or are easy and natural for me?

_____
_____
_____
_____
_____
_____
_____
_____
_____
_____
_____
_____
_____
_____
_____
_____
_____

List your strengths in one column and your passions in another column. Draw lines linking each strength to one or more passions.

List Your Requirements & Non-Negotiables

Possible non-negotiables include:

starting salary, location, great benefits, close to your family, specific job title, easy commute, number of vacation days, or autonomy in projects.

Write your list of non-negotiables and then see how it compares to your current and previous work roles.

What will you fight for to find fulfillment?

What do you need in your future work?

Discover Your Motivators

What has consistently motivated you in a work or project environment and hopefully across many teams or organizations?

What do I need my future career or position to provide for me?

What part of this work or hobby will bring me joy and fulfillment?

What list of boxes must be checked for you to want to do this?

_____
_____
_____
_____
_____
_____
_____
_____
_____
_____
_____
_____
_____
_____
_____

Work Environment

Think about where you want to work. Describing your ideal work-from-home office is a wonderful place to start as opportunities for employees to work partly (or entirely) from home increase.

What is your ideal work from home office?

Where Do You Want to Work

List where you find yourself the most productive... office, home, shared office, co-working space, outside, in the field... be specific and descriptive.

Describe the ideal location (rural, urban, suburban, city, street, neighborhood) and commute (long or short, public transportation, bike, walk, drive, none!).

Is it located near a specific store, restaurant, school, or gym?

What type of windows and lighting are important to you?

List the lighting, furniture, plants, decorations, or interior design that you are most attracted to and inspired by.

Describe the team of individuals you will be in contact with throughout the day both in person and virtually via phone, computer, or video call.

_____
_____
_____
_____
_____
_____
_____
_____
_____
_____
_____
_____
_____
_____
_____
_____

List a summary of your preferences from the lists above. Circle three items from your work-space wish lists above that you can't live without.

- Physical description

- Location

- Human Factor/Co-workers

- Technology or other tools you need

- Office Perks

Finding a Perfect Match

The purpose of this exercise is to help you use online search tools to find jobs.

Insert your skills into a job hunt site. What job openings does the site suggest for you?

Consider your favorite jobs from your past work experience and pretend you are offered a promotion to a higher level of responsibility or an even more enjoyable description of responsibilities. Consider what a step up would look like if you moved to the top company in your industry or even a competitor.

What would a big promotion look like?

LIST jobs and/or hobbies – real or invented – for which you would be a great candidate.

_____
_____
_____
_____
_____
_____
_____
_____
_____
_____
_____
_____
_____
_____
_____

Summarize all the job descriptions or roles into one list from the above searches. After each position, briefly list what makes you a suitable candidate for the job or perfect to start/continue this hobby.

Job 1:

Why would you be great for this job?

Job 2:

Why would you be great for this job?

Job 3:

Why would you be great for this job?

Dream Job/Hobby

For the dream job exercise, use the information you gathered from the earlier exercises in this chapter to summarize a perfect job for you. This exercise offers a rare opportunity to do the reverse of a typical job hunt. Instead of searching for a job opportunity/description, you create the ideal one for your career goals. The point of this exercise is to create a rubric to compare jobs you may apply to while job hunting with what your ideal job would look like.

What is your dream job? NOTES:

_____
_____
_____
_____
_____
_____
_____
_____
_____
_____
_____
_____
_____
_____
_____
_____

Complete this for a hobby if that is your focus at this time.

Imagine you are working at your ideal dream job. Where do you see yourself? Where do you want to be? Dream Big!

Where is a stretch position that is very attractive to you? It may be in the same industry or corporation. It may be in a new area you want to learn more about.

What makes this opportunity attractive to you? What financial gains, perks, benefits, responsibilities, time, recognition, future opportunities, and logical next steps will this position allow you to pursue?

_____
_____
_____
_____
_____
_____
_____
_____
_____
_____
_____
_____
_____
_____
_____
_____
_____
_____

Work/Hobby environment: Describe the job setting you want, focusing on what is most important to you.

Chapter 6 Find Your Place: Seek Where You Are Needed in the World

Where you are most needed in the world? Seek where you can make a difference in the world. To find where you are truly needed requires the demanding work of researching before taking steps or deciding.

Target Marketing Basics

Your target market is someone that can offer you a position, recommend you for an interview, or show you how to become a more attractive candidate for a specific job.

Who do you know in your network of connections that could help you find a job?

_____
_____
_____
_____
_____
_____
_____
_____
_____
_____
_____
_____
_____
_____
_____
_____
_____
_____

Chapter 6 Exercises

Target Marketing for Career Seekers
Basic techniques to find your high value career helpers.

A target market in this situation is someone who needs to hire, collaborate with, or knows the right person to connect you with that will hire you. An ideal target market during a job hunt is someone needing or looking for a professional with your skillset and abilities.

List the qualities of your ideal employer:

Who have been your best-fit employers in the past?

_____
_____
_____
_____
_____
_____
_____
_____
_____
_____
_____
_____
_____
_____
_____
_____
_____
_____

What problem do your unique abilities solve and who needs your abilities the most?

Why do past employers love your skills and abilities?

Who else have you worked with that has a similar resume?

Who else could become part of your target market that isn't already?

Where can you find employers that use people like you? List locations offline/online, geographic areas, industries, companies, and organizations.

_____
_____
_____
_____
_____
_____
_____
_____
_____
_____
_____
_____
_____
_____
_____
_____

Target Market Communication Plan

To successfully communicate you need to know what to say, where to say it, and the right time to reach a person that can help you get your next job.

What forms of social media and traditional communication do they enjoy and use regularly? (Notice where the company or specific individuals engage online or in person at events.

Who do they follow or industry periodicals they are likely to read? What organizations do they belong to or believe in?

What advertising and news are they motivated by: types of content, message type, form of media?

_____
_____
_____
_____
_____
_____
_____
_____
_____
_____
_____
_____
_____
_____
_____
_____
_____

What is the cost in time and money to reach your target market? (Consider the amount of travel, time, and expense to attend a conference or webinar, join an organization, or meet for coffee or lunch. Geographic or other restrictions may limit who and how often you can reach your target market directly. Get creative with virtual coffees or even phone calls to connect with your target market.)

What resources or training do you need to reach your target market?

Which resources or training are in your personal brand marketing budget and are likely to succeed?

When is your target market most likely to be open to communicate with you or any candidate for a role in their organization or to talk to you about your next steps in their industry?

What topics could you use to create content in the form of a blog post, journal article or social media post that is similar to what they are most likely to read and react to in a positive way?

Target Market Listening Plan

As you work on communicating with your target market, use comments, social feeds, social media listening, and trusted colleagues to hear what your target market thinks of your personal brand and message.

Start by analyzing the current industry or field that you are in and then move to industries in which you are considering pursuing a career. Listen to understand what topics are important to the people that you may eventually work with and for.

What social media do you need to follow to keep up with your industry?

What influencers are the most important to listen to in order to keep up with your industry?

Who else do you need to be listening to: publications, podcasts, experts?

_____
_____
_____
_____
_____
_____
_____
_____
_____
_____
_____
_____
_____
_____
_____
_____

Opportunity Lists by Industry

What industries have opportunities for you? If you can fill an unmet need for which people are willing to pay, there is a job for you. Be open to possibilities.

List the industries you are interested as a job source.

Career Track

Create a list of specific companies or organizations that have or could have the perfect job/position for you. Again, start with your current industry and then spread out to other possibilities.

_____
_____
_____
_____
_____
_____
_____
_____
_____
_____
_____
_____
_____
_____
_____
_____

Lifestyle track

List communities that center around your ideal hobby/lifestyle.

These could be online or in-person communities with actual buildings or people loosely bound together by a common interest. Companies that produce the equipment or locations for the hobby may function as a moderator or central location for the group so start with your favorite tools, equipment, or places.

List as many organizations, conventions, events, or companies that you can with ties to the hobby or lifestyle.

Job Post for Career Track Template

After creating a list of organizations, visit their websites or job boards that list open opportunities. Combine these to get an idea of what a perfect job would be for you. Career consultants, coaches, and headhunters use this technique to help them search for jobs with a higher chance that you will accept the position. Create the job offer you couldn't refuse.

Looking for a candidate for the position of _____ (job title) at

_____ (company).

The position will be located at _____ (workplace location).

Position responsibilities include:

Benefits include:

Candidate must have these educational requirements:

Fun and Fulfilling Careers One Question at a Time: Workbook

These skills:

This experience:

Other details for the ideal job post:

Sales Pitch for Lifestyle track

Consider how your ideal hobby could become a part-time job or side hustle. Small (and large) businesses often start out as hobbies. Create the ultimate sales pitch. Imagine you are in front of a room full of venture capitalists. Investors with money that are looking for the ideal small business to launch into reality are sitting right in front of you. Imagine, these investors are lined up just waiting to hear about how your hobby could be turned into a successful and thriving business.

What would you do or say that would make your product or service stand out?

What would they look for in what you say about your business to believe that you have what it takes?

What are the areas you would never compromise on if they wanted to invest?

What would you make them promise they wouldn't change if you sold them your side business?

How many sales or what size profit margin would you need to know that this is more than a hobby?

Additional factors to consider:

_____
_____
_____
_____
_____
_____
_____
_____
_____
_____
_____
_____
_____
_____

Interviewing an Expert

Interview at least two people who are currently employed or are an expert in each of your dream jobs/hobbies. Use the **Interviewing an Expert Template** below.

IMPORTANT: Send an email or note to thank them for their time afterward.

Create a list of potential people to interview:

Person being interviewed:

Contact phone number and email:

Current title position:

Company/business type:

How do you know them or who gave you their contact information?

Questions for the person:

Why did you choose your job/hobby?

How did you get here? Experience, education, networking, innovative thinking, opportunity, personal relationship, or connection.

What do you love most about the job/hobby?

What do you wish was better or different?

Finally, what advice would you give to someone considering this type of position?

Person being interviewed:

Contact phone number and email:

Current title position:

Company/business type:

How do you know them or who gave you their contact information?

Questions for the person:

Why did you choose your job/hobby?

How did you get here? Experience, education, networking, innovative thinking, opportunity, personal relationship, or connection.

What do you love most about the job/hobby?

What do you wish was better or different?

Finally, what advice would you give to someone considering this type of position?

Person being interviewed:

Contact phone number and email:

Current title position:

Company/business type:

How do you know them or who gave you their contact information?

Questions for the person:

Why did you choose your job/hobby?

How did you get here? Experience, education, networking, innovative thinking, opportunity, personal relationship, or connection.

What do you love most about the job/hobby?

What do you wish was better or different?

Finally, what advice would you give to someone considering this type of position?

Researching Company or Community Analysis

For each company or community, fill out as many of the following sections as possible. Ask questions of human resources, former or current employees, or research online in social media sites and industry publications. Use the space below or a spreadsheet or table to keep the information organized. Use the **Researching a Company Template** below.

Note: These questions are also useful during a job interview or in conversation with a potential employer to help you get to know the company, demonstrate a high level of interest in the company, and allow you to focus on more in-depth questions to ask your interviewer that will make you stand out from other candidates.

List the companies you wish to research:

Company 1 name:

Who are their customers? What is their relationship with customers?

What products or services do they offer?

Who are their competitors?

SWOT analysis: What are their Strengths, Weaknesses, Opportunities, and Threats?

What unique niche does the company fill in their field?

Where are they located?

What is their social media presence? (Platforms, online chatter, positive or negative)

What is the culture like? (Talk to an HR person, online culture measurements or current/former employee)

What is their Mission (Vision) Statement? (What does the company do and stand for?)

Company 1 name:

What is their financial situation? (Any red flags or concerns)

What positions within the company are they looking to fill? Look at all open positions as this may indicate an area that they are growing or having difficulty finding good candidates.

What is the contact information for Human Resources and hiring team?

Company 2 name:

Who are their customers? What is their relationship with customers?

What products or services do they offer?

Who are their competitors?

SWOT analysis: What are their Strengths, Weaknesses, Opportunities, and Threats?

Company 2 name:

What unique niche does the company fill in their field?

Where are they located?

What is their social media presence? (Platforms, online chatter, positive or negative)

What is the culture like? (Talk to an HR person, online culture measurements or current/former employee)

What is their Mission (Vision) Statement? (What does the company do and stand for?)

Company 2 name:

What is their financial situation? (Any red flags or concerns)

What positions within the company are they looking to fill? Look at all open positions as this may indicate an area that they are growing or having difficulty finding good candidates.

What is the contact information for Human Resources and hiring team?

Company 3 name:

Who are their customers? What is their relationship with customers?

What products or services do they offer?

Who are their competitors?

SWOT analysis: What are their Strengths, Weaknesses, Opportunities, and Threats?

Company 3 name:

What unique niche does the company fill in their field?

Where are they located?

What is their social media presence? (Platforms, online chatter, positive or negative)

What is the culture like? (Talk to an HR person, online culture measurements or current/former employee)

What is their Mission (Vision) Statement? (What does the company do and stand for?)

Company 3 name:

What is their financial situation? (Any red flags or concerns)

What positions within the company are they looking to fill? Look at all open positions as this may indicate an area that they are growing or having difficulty finding good candidates.

What is the contact information for Human Resources and hiring team?

Lifestyle Track

Examine and research organizations, foundations, events, and clubs that celebrate and are centered around your favorite hobby. Attend conventions, conferences, masterminds, and online webinars for that industry Ask the questions above in the career track about each club or organization to learn which may be worth getting to know better.

Where can you find a community of people with similar interests to yours?

Part Three:
Communicating and Maintaining Your Personal Brand

For Chapter 7, we will map out a strategic plan to help you share and communicate your personal brand. Prepare to create an actual action list with time frames and goals. By the end of Chapter 7, you will have created a prioritized list of action items that will guide you and prepare you step by step for your greatest opportunities for fulfillment.

Finally, in Chapter 8, I have included recommendations for updating and maintaining your personal brand.

NOTES:

Chapter 7 Creating Your Strategic Personal Brand Plan: Specific Tasks and Actions to Achieve Your Ideal Work and Life

In creating your strategic personal brand plan, remember to be patient. The time you invest in this pursuit will pay off in more than just success in your field, it will also pay off in your life.

Failure as a Requirement

Be prepared for interviews, the next time a recruiter asks you directly, "Tell me about a time you failed." own the question. Share the life lessons, strategies, and new directions that the experience helped you discover. Let the lessons of failure guide you to the next ideal job or position. Remind the interviewer that without failure the ideal candidate would not be available for that next opening.

List times you have failed and learned from the failure.

NOTES:

_____
_____
_____
_____
_____
_____
_____
_____
_____
_____
_____
_____
_____
_____
_____
_____
_____

Social Media Pyramid

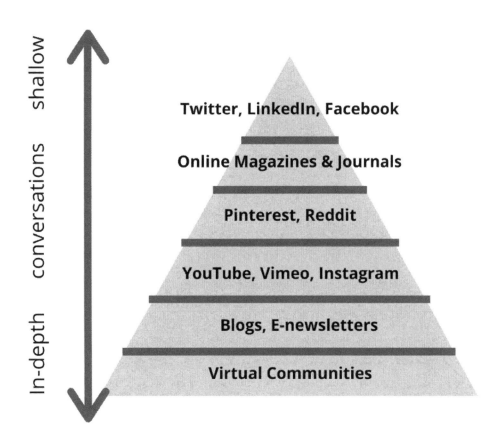

The Social Media Pyramid lists the most commonly used forms of social media in a format that describes the depth of discussions on specific topics.

The top of the pyramid represents broad reach in numbers of audience and the lowest part ot the pyramid represents fewer but more targeted audience members.

The higher the platform is listed in the pyramid, the more shallow the discussions will be for a specific topic. With the most in-depth discussions occurring near the bottom of the pyramid.

This version created by Heather H. Bennett

Social Media Pyramid Diagram

Social Media

The best advice I give to clients about social media is to only invest time and money in the social media platforms that (1) resonate with you, (2) are directly tied to communicating your message to your target markets, and (3) communicate that message in the most effective way. Otherwise, you are wasting your time.

What social media platforms do you spend time on now? Why?

What social media platforms are being used to discuss topics of importance in your field or industry?

_____
_____
_____
_____
_____
_____
_____
_____
_____
_____
_____
_____
_____
_____
_____
_____

LinkedIn

Best used for: Job hunters, sales professionals, business development and B2B (Business to business) sharing of business and industry related topics and discussions. Sharing job experience and acting as a live resume. Establishing thought leadership and social proof of professional knowledge.

Who is your ideal audience for your LinkedIn Profile?

What do they need to know about you from your LinkedIn?

Blogs/Podcasts/Vlogs

Best used for: Driving traffic to your website to sell your products or services.

What topics could you write, film, or record about on a regular basis:

Website

Best used for: Sharing information, selling products, or encouraging the visitor to your website to connect with you. Most importantly, it is used to help a visitor solve a problem.

Do you need a website? Ask yourself how important it is for you to establish yourself as an authority in a specific topic or expertise or to demonstrate your thought leadership?

Does your business depend on name or brand recognition of you?

Email Newsletters

Best used for: Keeping you and your personal brand top of mind for your audience, followers, and for consumers to drive them to buy your products and/or services.

Consider whether a simple monthly email newsletter to your subscribers could help with announcing new products, events or other information that would help your career and business.

Other social media platforms and opportunities:

Where else could you communicate your personal brand? Technology is constantly changing how we interact with each other. New communication platforms come and go. Be on the watch for what others in your industry are using to communicate.

Chapter 7 Exercises

The exercises in Chapter 7 are designed to create a specific action plan. Your Strategic Personal Brand Plan will consist of actions listed with due dates to keep you on track. By completing each action, you will get closer and closer to reaching your goals. For each of the sections below, write a plan and action steps with dates to complete for each one.

1. Reread your personal brand statement, ideal job description, and advice from experts. What would you change, remove, or add?

2. What training or skills do you need to do this job, hobby or live your lifestyle with excellence? What skills do you need to improve or learn? What training or skills do you need to stand out from the competition for what you want? What skills do you need to brush up on or receive training to excel in your lifestyle? Consider apprenticeships, internships, online courses, formal course work, webinars, group learning, and individual training.

3. Who is your "in" to the industry? Who is your inspiration in this lifestyle? Who are the influencers? Do you know someone from college, or even your professional, or social circles that could help you learn more about this hobby or lifestyle? Find at least one person who has been doing this hobby for at least five years to act as a mentor. Consider your business network, convention connections, company sports teams, LinkedIn contacts, other tangential companies that collaborate with the company directly, faith or school communities, social media groups, and your personal network.

4. Update your resume and LinkedIn to reflect your personal brand so you are prepared to share what you want. Create and practice aloud your elevator speech with a trusted friend or colleague to explain what you are seeking in an ideal job or hobby. Consider the elevator speech as a more polished version of what you would say when meeting someone at a party.

5. Keep up to date on industry news through communities, publications, webinars, conventions, conferences, Twitter, LinkedIn, blogs, Reddit, and key word searches.

6. List your action items in chronological order. Specify the dates to have each accomplished. Hold yourself accountable. Make a visual reminder that you check daily or weekly to keep inspired about your goals. Include reminders in your calendar with notifications or write the tasks in a To Do list. Think about how you are going to fund your new venture or hobby. An activity that stays in budget is a lot more enjoyable.

7. Optimize your performance. What would excellence look like? What makes someone exceptional or an expert? What level of performance would bring you great fulfillment? Sometimes excellence does not equal happiness or fulfillment. For a hobby, focus on excellence only if that will bring you enjoyment while preparing for or doing the hobby.

8. Make necessary course corrections. What changes or updates in your action plan do you need to make to stay on course and keep moving towards the career and life goals you talked about in Chapter 1?

9. Consider whether this is the greatest impact you could have on the world. Where else might your talents have a broader or deeper reach? Does this hobby or lifestyle fulfill at least one of your top goals in life? A hobby does not need to fulfill a life goal or make the world a better place. The important part of a hobby is to bring you enjoyment. If it happens to make the world a better place or fulfill a life goal, that is a bonus.

Personal Brand Strategy

Fill out the following statements considering everything you have learned about yourself while reading this book. Feel free to flip back and forth through your notes to better understand which of your words to fill in each blank. Act to make your life fulfilling!

OPTION 1: Personal Branding taught me the following about myself

I learned I want to spend more time doing:

    1.

    2.

    3.

    because they help me....

    or give me joy through using my unique talents and skills.

In the future, I want to do:

I want to be:

I want to spend more time doing:

In 3-5 years, I see myself doing:

with this organization

so, I can achieve my goals of:

OPTION 2: Elevator Speech

Another way to write your personal brand plan is to create an elevator speech. Use this short less-than-one-minute speech to share the following information at a networking event or conference. The elevator speech should include: your name, what you do for a living in easy-to-understand terms, what you need help with, how you can help others and finally a direct Call to Action (CTA). The CTA should be specific. List how to contact or connect with you and have time parameters within a month or the next year. See the diagram to get started.

NOTES:

Elevator Pitch Components Diagram

Write out your Elevator Pitch using the Elevator Pitch Template below.

1. Introduction

2. Goals

3. Call-to-Action

4. Stories that can showcase your abilities

Accountability Chart for Your Personal Brand Strategy
To reach my career and life goals, I need to accomplish the following actions:

In 1 month, I need to: ….

In 6 months, I need to: ….

In 1 year, I need to: ….

I will continue to find time to take care of myself and reevaluate my personal branding statement as I grow and change. I will create a new action plan when what I am doing with my life is not bringing me joy and fulfillment or conflicts with helping me reach my goals.

Chapter 8 Keeping Your Personal Brand Strong: Checkups, Maintenance, and Updates

Congratulations! You have completed the hard work for your personal brand by:
- getting to know yourself and your personal brand authentically,
- writing a core description,
- creating a personal branding statement and/or elevator speech,
- crafting messages and templates to communicate your personal brand, and
- designing an action plan of tasks to reach your personal goals

Networking with a Purpose

What is your purpose or purposes for networking?

Who do you want to talk to?

How can they help you?

How can you help them?

_____
_____
_____
_____
_____
_____
_____
_____
_____
_____
_____
_____
_____
_____
_____
_____
_____

Networking from Multiple Viewpoints

Before attending a networking event, think about why the event is taking place and answer the following questions.

What is the purpose of the event from the perspective of the organization or person planning the event?

What do you and the other attendees of the networking event hope to gain from attending the event?

Make a List of Networking Events you plan to attend in the next 3-6 months

_____
_____
_____
_____
_____
_____
_____
_____
_____
_____
_____
_____
_____
_____
_____
_____

Take Time to Celebrate

. What are ways you can celebrate your and your teams' achievements?

_____
_____
_____
_____
_____
_____
_____
_____
_____
_____
_____
_____
_____
_____
_____
_____
_____
_____
_____

How to Celebrate

- Call a friend and share your news

- Buy that treat you have been waiting for the right moment to purchase. This could be new shoes, a dessert or meal at your favorite restaurant, sports or technical equipment, a book, ticket to a concert, play or movie, the workout class or coaching session you have been wanting to join. What have you been wishing for and waiting for the right moment of accomplishment to acquire?

- Book a trip for an overnight or weekend away. (See the topic on Planning is More than Half the Fun for why you should book at least a few weeks in advance.)

- Take a mental health afternoon off from work to go to a museum or have a picnic.

- Throw a party (themed or not, big, or small, with or without decorations, virtual or in person): Tea, costume, karaoke, beach, online via Facebook Portal or Zoom.

- Book a spa treatment.

- Schedule online gaming with multiple friends for a weeknight for an hour or two.

Making the World a Better Place

Ask yourself am I making the biggest impact I can in the world? Where can I be a contributor to making the world a better place?

How will what I do make the world a more efficient or more amazing place?

_____
_____
_____
_____
_____
_____
_____
_____
_____
_____
_____
_____
_____
_____
_____

Chapter 8 Exercises

Pre-Networking Checklist

A quick way to make the time you spend networking worthwhile is to prepare mentally before the event. Take a few minutes to use this pre-networking checklist to prepare for your next event.

- What is your purpose for attending the event?

- Who are the people you hope to meet?

- What help do you need? What is your "ask"?

- What help can you offer to those you meet?

Social Media Checklist for Personal Brands

A weekly social media checklist allows you to prioritize time to focus on your social media without being drawn into the spiral of spending hours reading posts and replying.

Weekly List (Only do the tasks for social media platforms you have committed to being engaged in. Ignore the social media platforms you do not want to use.)

Daily Tasks
- Scan the subject line of all work-related emails at the start, middle and end of the workday
- Check notifications for Twitter once per day during the workweek only to respond to direct messages, Retweet posts of interest and thank new followers

Weekly Tasks
- Check, read, and respond to messages or requests to connect on LinkedIn.
- Check Instagram (and/or Pinterest), post one post.
- If a major event occurs or a topic is highly trending, check your schedule and posts to make sure your posts are not seen as insensitive or inappropriate.

Monthly Tasks
- Check and engage with Facebook.
- Set aside 2-4 hours to create posts for all social media platforms to use over the next month.
- Schedule ahead posts for the next 30 days using a scheduler (you may need to do more than once a month depending on the scheduler limitations) or upgrade to an unlimited paid plan to schedule months in advance.

Quarterly Tasks
- Update your customer relationship management software with new connections or current information on current connections.
- Update your content files.

Annual Tasks
- Get a new headshot to update your profile on all social media (If you don't have time or the funds to hire a professional photographer, use your or a friend's phone with a great filter, natural light, and a solid color shirt).
- Review the profile wording or description on all of your social media to keep updated and authentic.

- Set goals for social media and create a plan for number, type, and scheduling of posts for each platform.
- Review your technology needs and equipment, buy new equipment to make managing social media easy.
- Review software to improve or switch to a new software or plan if you have outgrown your current one.
- Consider outsourcing content creation or posting if your budget allows.

Social media is a tool to help us communicate with others. Focusing on the message, the audience, and purpose of each post will help keep the time you spend on social media manageable. Planning what to post and when to post will give you more time for what you are truly passionate about.

NOTES:

Create your own customized Weekly Checklist based on the ideas listed above

Daily

Weekly

_____
_____
_____
_____
_____
_____
_____
_____
_____
_____
_____
_____
_____
_____
_____

Quarterly

Yearly

Timeline Planner

A Timeline Planner is a productivity tool designed to help plan when projects will actually get accomplished.

This tool works best after you have already completed the Time Map exercise. By having a Time Map of all of the parts of your life, it will be easier to strategically place the different tasks needed to complete your responsibilities and prepare for events that occur throughout the year. There are many different ways to create a Timeline Planner. Find a method that works for you to get your Timeline Planner completed.

Timeline Planner Example

TIME LINE PLANNER

A productivity tool to help plan when projects will actually get accomplished. Use this planner after completing the Time Map exercise to organize how to fulfill commitments, accomplish projects and reach goals this year.

Category	JAN	FEB	MAR	APR	MAY	JUN	JUL	AUG	SEP	OCT	NOV	DEC
FAMILY				Spring Break				Vacation				Winter Break
WORK: MAIN			Q1 Report			Q2 Report			Q3 Report			Q4 Report
WORK: PROJECT A	New Product Launch						Product Annual Review Strategy Planning			Choose new product line		
WORK: TEAM			Prepare for Annual Meeting	Annual Meeting Team Retreat								Team Review
SELF CARE	Monthly Meeting with Personal Trainer and Nutritionist											
FRIENDS						College Friend Weekend						Holiday Party
VOLUNTEERING			Fundraising Gala						Fall 5K fundraiser			
CAREER	Update Resume Personal Brand					Industry Conference		New Head Shots		Alumni Event	Content Calendar	
SIDE HUSTLE				Due Diligence					Loan Application		Finalize website	

copyright by Heather H. Bennett

Draw out a rough draft of your Timeline Planner for Year

Draw out a rough draft of your Timeline Planner for Year _____

Conclusion

Congratulations! By completing the exercises in this workbook and contemplating the various topics discussed throughout, you have worked hard to better understand how to find fun and fulfillment in your life and career.

After reading the book, Fun and Fulfilling Careers One Question at a Time and doing the exercises in this workbook, I encourage you to act to reach your goals and to embrace your unique personal brand. Follow the plan you developed to find the best opportunities out there for you. I wish you continued energy, motivation, and inspiration.

Revisit and redo the exercises at critical moments in your journey, remembering that we are all a work in progress.

As you continue your personal brand journey remember these two things: One, be true to your own authentic personal brand. Two, try to make the world a better place by helping others.

Life is too fragile and short to not live it to the fullest. Why not do so in a way that makes it fulfilling!

I hope every day brings you more fun and fulfillment!

Acknowledgements

This workbook would not exist without a lot of help from God and many, many kind friends.

Thank you to my professional board of directors for their champion level support, wise words, and even wiser questions.

Thank you to the many friends, clients and colleagues that inspired and discussed the concepts in this workbook, listened patiently, evaluated exercises, and helped me with research.

Thank you to my dear family from coast to coast and the wonderful nonprofit organizations that give me the opportunity to make the world a better place.

To my kids and my awesome husband…Thank you for putting up with my frantic attempts to find time to write another book. Please know none of this would be possible without you.

About the Author

Heather H. Bennett is the author of the Amazon Bestseller, *Fun and Fulfilling Careers One Question at a Time*, a marketing strategist, board director and personal brand expert with 20+ years of experience, including marketing brands such as VO5, Vaseline, Ponds, Pyrex, and Claussen Pickles. Drawing from her MBA, Social Media Marketing Certification, and multiple Board Governance Certifications, she coaches her clients to create strong, authentic, and unique brands through her business, Creative Brand Coach.

Working jobs as varied as assembly line worker, national chain restaurant host, research biologist, brand manager, small business owner, and board of directors' member has shaped Heather's unique perspective on personal branding and careers. Her personal branding method has been shared at workshops, podcasts, and webinars.

Heather lives in Chicago, Illinois with her husband and four children, where she enjoys volunteering for non-profits, reading mystery novels and spending as much time as possible outside swimming, kayaking, and hiking.

To connect with Heather about marketing, social media, board governance and personal branding, visit her website: www.creativebrandcoach.net

Made in the USA
Monee, IL
11 January 2023

25062985R00081